David Jaffin

# Spring Poems
# Shadowings

First published in the United Kingdom in 2021 by
Shearsman Books
50 Westons Hill Drive
Emersons Green
Bristol BS16 7DF

Shearsman Books Ltd Registered Office
30–31 St. James Place, Mangotsfield, Bristol BS16 9JB
*(this address not for correspondence)*

www.shearsman.com

978-1-84861-401-7

Distributed for Shearsman Books in the U. S. A.
by Small Press Distribution, 1341 Seventh Avenue, Berkeley, CA 94710
E-Mail orders@spdbooks.org
www.spdbooks.org

*Production, composition, & cover design:* Edition Wortschatz,
a service of Neufeld Verlag, Cuxhaven/Germany
E-Mail info@edition-wortschatz.de, www.edition-wortschatz.de

*Title illustration:*
"Würmtal beim Starnberger See",
by Hannelore Bäumler, München

Printed in Germany

# Contents

7

With continuing thanks for
Marina Moisel
preparing
this manuscript

and to Hanni Bäumler
for her well-placed
photograph

If I had to classify my poetry, it could best be done through the classical known "saying the most by using the least". The aim is thereby set: transparency, clarity, word-purity. Every word must carry its weight in the line and the ultimate aim is a unity of sound, sense, image and idea. Poetry, more than any other art, should seek for a unity of the senses, as the French Symbolists, the first poetic modernists, realized through the interchangeability of the senses: "I could hear the colors of her dress." One doesn't hear colors, but nevertheless there is a sensual truth in such an expression.

Essential is "saying the most by using the least". Compression is of the essence. And here are some of my most personal means of doing so turning verbs into nouns and the reverse, even within a double-context "Why do the leaves her so ungenerously behind". Breaking words into two or even three parts to enable both compression and the continuing flow of meaning. Those words must be placed back together again, thereby revealing their inner structure-atomising.

One of my critics rightly said: "Jaffin's poetry is everywhere from one seemingly unrelated poem to the next." Why? Firstly because of my education and interests trained at New York University as a cultural and intellectual historian. My doctoral dissertation on historiography emphasizes the necessary historical continuity. Today we often judge the past with the mind and mood of the present, totally contrary to their own historical context. I don't deny the past-romanticism and classical but integrate them within a singular modern context of word-usage and sensibility. Musically that would place me within the "classical-romantic tradition" of Haydn, Mozart, Mendelssohn, Brahms and Nielsen but at the very modern end of that tradition.

My life historically is certainly exceptional. My father was a prominent New York Jewish lawyer. The law never interested me, but history always did. A career as a cultural-intellectual historian was mine-for-the-asking, but I rejected historical relativism. That led me to a marriage with a devout German lady – so I took to a calling of Jesus-the-Jew in post-Auschwitz Germany. For ca. two decades I wrote and lectured all over Germany on Jesus the Jew. Thereby my knowledge and understanding of both interlocked religions became an essential part of my being. History, faith and religion two sides of me but also art, classical music and literature were of essential meaning – so many poems on poetry, classical music and painting.

Then Rosemarie and I have been very happily married for 59 years now. Impossible that a German and Jew could be so happily married so shortly after the war? I've written love poems for her, hundreds and hundreds over those 59 years, not only the love poems, as most are, of the first and often unfulfilling passion, but "love and marriage go together like a horse and carriage". Perhaps too prosaic for many poets?

When did I become a poet? My sister Lois wrote reasonably good poetry as an adolescent. I, only interested in sports until my Bar Mitzvah, a tournament tennis and table-tennis player, coached baseball and basketball teams, also soccer.

My sister asked whether I'd ever read Dostoyevsky. I'd only read John R. Tunis sports books and the sports section of the *New York Times* so I answered "in which sports was he active?" She said, rather condescendingly, "If you haven't read Dostoyevsky, you haven't lived." So I went to the library for the very first time and asked for a book by this Dostoyevsky. I received *Poor People*, his first book, that made him world famous. My mother shocked to see me reading and most especially a book about poor people said, "David, don't read that it will make you sad, unhappy – we, living in Scarsdale, weren't after all, poor people. From there it went quickly to my Tolstoy, Hardy and so on. In music it started with the hit parade, then *Lost in the Stars*, then the popular classics and with 15 or 16 my Haydn, Mozart, Schütz, Victoria … And then at Ann Arbor and NYU to my artists, most especially Giovanni Bellini, Van der Weyden, Georges de la Tour, Corot and Gauguin …

But it was Wallace Stevens' reading in the early 50s in the YMHA that set me off – he didn't read very well, but his 13 Ways of Looking at a Blackbird, Idea of Order at Key West, Two Letters (in *Poems Posthumous*), Peter Quince at the Clavier, The Snowman … and the excellent obituary in *Time* magazine plus the letter he answered some of my poems with compliments but "you must be your own hardest critic". That pre-determined my extremely self-critical way with a poem. Please don't believe that prolific means sloppy, for I'm extremely meticulous with each and every poem.

My poems were published in the order written and I'm way ahead of any counting... The poem is a dialogical process as everything in life. The words come to me not from me, and if they strike or possibly join-a-union then I become desparate, read long-winded poets like Paz to set me off – he's very good at odd times. Those poems need my critical mood-mind as much as I need their very specially chosen words – not the "magic words" of the romantics, but the cleansed words of Jaffin – Racine used only 500 words. My words too are a specially limited society, often used, but in newly-felt contexts.

O something very special: I have a terrible poetic memory. If I had a good one as presumably most poets, I'd write say one poem about a butterfly, and every time I see/saw a butterfly it would be that one, that poem. But I forget my poems, so each butterfly, lizard, squirrel... is other-placed, other-mooded, other-worded, other-Jaffined. That's the main reason why I am most certainly the most prolific of all poets.

Shakespeare is the greatest of us: his sonnets live most from the fluency and density of his language. I advise all future poets to keep away from his influence and the poetic greatness of The Bible.

*Yours truly*
*David Jaffin*

P. S.: As a preacher the truth (Christ) should become straight-lined, timelessly so, but as a poet it's quite different. What interests me most are those contradictions which live deeply within all of us, not only in theory, but daily in the practice. And then the romantics have led me to those off-sided thoroughly poetic truths that mysteriously not knowing where that darkened path will lead us.

*Poems Opus 101*

## Prelude *(4)*

*a) Am I now*

with opus 101

in sight com
pletely empt

*b) ied-out or*

is the creat

ive process
one of refilling

what's been

*c) taken-out*

until the new
ly called poem

s waiting in
line once a

*d) gain and I*

as always de

pendent on
their self–

fulfilling
word.

## May 7 an (4)

*a) almost perfect*

picture-book

day the sky
a self-guaran

*b) teeing blue*

almost no wind

upsetting this
motionless

heavenly over

*c) heard response*

The go-ahead
signal set for

a newly track

*d) ed into the*

unknown realm
s of poetical

ly elusive-un
certaintie

s.

## Some of these *(4)*

*a) poems may seem*

out-of-bound

s for many de
vout Christian

*b) readers Other*

s for those

always politi
cally- intent

But the poem

*c) itself must de*

cide (perhap
s with a slight

nudge here or

*d) there from the*

poet's over
sight) of its

specially-
chosen route.

## *Will there e (3)*

*a) ver become a*

post-Corona

era or is
that invis

*b) ible world-*

wide virus

continual
ly changing

what we'd
come to call

*c) "normal" a*

word-concept

that's still
plaguing serious

ly-minded ther
apist

s.

## When safety- *(8)*

*a) first require*

s a (temporary)

closing of the
borders between


*b) countries state*

s counties even

families then
Corona may be

come a future
model for an


*c) oncoming encom*

passing dictator

ship sailing
its own pre

establish

*d) ing so called*

"temporary"
rule-chang

es That the
Corona virus con

*e) tinues to have*

a lesser effect

on those post–
Communistic

East–German

*f) landscaping*

s caused by
their open-spac

ed lesser popu
lated areas but

*g) perhaps also*

by Corona's un

spoken sympathy
for what's re

*h) created in the*

image of a

similar author
itarian raison

d'être.


## No doubt our *(5)*

*a) faith continue*

s to blossom

through the
blood of world–

*b) wide Christian*

martyrers And

while most–of–
us prefer liv

ing in a com


*c) fortably free*

democratic
ally prosper

ous land That
creates (if we'


*d) re honest with*

ourselves) an

inner devide
between what

we personal

*e) ly prefer and*

our Lord's
very-much o

therwise-
way.


## That what' (2)

*a) s aestheti*

cally so fine

ly wrought as
a spider's

web by no mean


*b) s guarantee*

s that its
usage will re

veal what's e
qually fine-

feeling.

# When two (4)

*a) large beauti*

fully color–

designed bird
s landed at

*b) opposite end*

s of my bal

cony I immed
iately suspect

ed they were

*c) spying-out the*

whereabout
s of my 5

highly regard
ed nuts also

*d) balcony-wise*

situated be

fore my very
suggestive

eye-length
s.

## *Still life* (3)

*a) Those 5 wal*

nuts have sat

so long on my
wooden bal


*b) cony in their*

inward suspend

ing quietude
s that they'

ve become a
genuine still


*c) life birthed*

in our dialog

ue of an un
spoken spirit

ual–companion
ship.

## When the first *(6)*

*a) word-selection*

feels a bit

uneasy doesn't
fit just–right

*b) upon rereading*

another – you

might call it
an intruder had

occupied its

*c) now permanent*

ly desired
home-base My

eldest sister
presented to her

*d) father a first*

ling of a fu

ture husband-
acceptibil

ity He made my


*e) father's Harvard*

Law School quali
fications but

my sister's 2nd
choice – not


*f) that kind of*

second–choice

remained there
to stay a life–

timed together
ness.

## Their garden

punctuated
with tiny flo

wers express
ing perhaps a

communal desire
for a self-uni

fying voice.


## When the wind

s spoke all
the newly form

ed leaves be
came rewarded

with a
sanctifying

dance-like
answering–

response.

# Wind-shadow

s as if open
ing-out an

escape route
for some flee

ing mytholog
ical Greek-

goddess.


# 2<sup>nd</sup> Commandment *(Moses) (2)*

*a) It's difficult*

after so many

years of a
self-fulfill

ing marriage
to realise

that the o


*b) ther-half may*

continue to

harbour his or
her own exist

encial–prior
itie

s.

## The only (3)

*a) possible irre*

placable loss

for me would
be if Rosemarie

*b) died before*

me The loss

of each close
friend leave

s a big or

*c) bigger person*

al void but
not of the

same life–form
ing quality.

## One day *(3)*

*a) one of us*

will wake-

up to dis
cover the o

*b) ther won't*

because the

Angel of Death
had taken him

or her to a

*c) far distant*

land we have
n't been able

to map–out
until now.

## The funeral (7)

*a) of a believer*

should become

a joyful occas
ion as in Ire

*b) land because*

he or she

now's in a
timeless

heavenly

*c) better world*

without sin
pain and e

ven death it
self Each de

nomination

*d) seems to have*

carefully mark
ed reserve

seats up there
Jesus Himself

denied two of

*e) his apostel*

s such special
rights only

those who have
withstood daily

temptation


*f) s while liv*

ing daily
from Jesus'

forgiveness
may then dis

cover unnumber


*g) ed reserved*

seats bear
ing their new

ly accorded
name-sake.

## *Zooed Visit* (6)

*a) ing the zoo*

may open–out

for some Aesop
–like similar


*b) ities For Rose*

marie perhaps

the water–bound
dance–escort

ing seals For


*c) me those bury*

ing–their–head
s–in–the–sand Os

triches For
Raphael the time

*d) ly-sitting pro*

tective–lion

Last–but–not–
least for Andr

eas perhaps the
Prussian–like


*e) under-officer'*

s penguins …

But even more
important the

way those cur


*f) ious animal*

s imagine them
selves through

our strange
ly otherwise

behavior.

## Pain-demo *(5)*

*a) cracy I never*

quite realis
ed just how

democrati


*b) cally-inclin*

ed the part
s of my body

respond One day
the big toe


*c) on the other*

side from the

earlier paraly
sed one Now the

most chronical

*d) ly pained right*

shoulder
On some rainy

days alternate

ly hip back
and the other-sid


*e) ed shoulder*

There-you-have-
it the pained-

democracy of
the over-80s.

## Can being marr *(3)*

*a) ied to a "bor*

der-line" set–

off a sick
ness tracked


*b) to its own*

most unhealthy

destination
Such "border–

lines" quest
ion the very


*c) raison d'être*

of others

most especial
ly those in

close daily–
contact.

# *Looking-deep-* *(2)*

*a) down into that*

voiceless

pond he felt
a darkly

trouble


*b) some-response*

somehow acti
vating most

necessary
safety–meas

ures.

## Budding *(2)*

*a) friendship*

s require as

newly plant
ed flower

s a most care


*b) fully tending*

hand to estab
lish the necess

ary depth for a
dialoguing

life-growth.


## This swell

ing green
s begun crowd

ing me in
from its ex

panding space-
indigenous

time-telling
s.

## Keeping-up *(4)*

### *a) with-the-time*

s has been

for centurie
s since the


### *b) so-called en*

lightenment

a speciality
of German liber

al theology
relativising


### *c) not only Jesus*

St. Paul and
basic bibli

cal theology
thereby leav

ing unanswer


### *d) ed the central*

questions of
life–itself

love and death'
s all–encompass

ing dominion.

## Practical *(3)*

*a) ly the whole*

world was caught

unprepared
for Corona'

*b) s deathly-sway*

Has that be

come a good
reason to

trust the judg

*c) ment of so-*

called expert
s who have

failed us so
often in the

past.

## How far can (3)

*a) history enable a*

people to change

its very raison–
d'être Is the

"New Germany"


*b) completely re*

fashioned or
for example

has a partly
endemic anti–

semetism aris


*c) en from the*

ashes of the
Third Reich

to reassert its
most menacing–

credential
s.

## Cultivated (4)

*a) She said with*

but a touch of

pride "we've
cultivated

*b) these flower*

s ourselve

s That word-
concept "culti

vated" remained
with me the en

*c) tire afternoon*

somewhere bet

ween artifi
cial and genuine

flowers but arti
ficially not

*d) naturally*

there Somehow

that inbetween
word implied "do

mesticated".

*I've been* (6)

    *a) brought-up*

    as I'm most

    certain as
    many before and

    *b) after distin*

    guishing between

    appearance
    what's gen

    uine quality-

    *c) wise But even*

    the late Michel
    angelo a devout

    Christian was
    taken-in by a

*d) beautifying*

presence perhaps

because he was
a sculptor and

painter Beauty re


*e) mains beauty*

whether for
appearance-

sake or on a


*f) deeper-level*

character and
personally

self-inhabit
ing.

# *Can one be* *(3)*

*a) come literate*

without read

ing books He
my weekend


*b) "driver"*

was an act

ive engineer
He remember

ed what he'


*c) d heard at*

the lecture
s became

bookless–liter
ate.

## With him (6)

a) there's almost

always an un

easy feeling
afterward


b) s This time

his brother'

s pain-controll
ed death didn'

t change his


c) own suicidal

decision That
was too-much-

out-of-bound
s for Rosemarie

*d) We got up and*

left well know

ing we'll re
turn again (if

*e) he's still a*

live) after de

cades of much–
the-same remind

ing (perhaps)
of my eldest sis

*f) ter's happy marr*

iage mostly ar

guing but in
their case as

a sign of accept
ing and loving.

## *Academic(4)*

*a) competancy's*

no measure for

political-qual
ity as little


*b) as for invent*

ive-original

ity Our "great
tycoons" remain

ed mostly with
out a high


*c) school diploma*

Despite I. Q.

tests there'
s no accurate

measure for in
telligence

*d) so varied as*

those numerous

parallel track
s to Grand Cen

tral Station.


## *Praise* (5)

*a) Beautiful women*

usually remain

particular
ly keen on


*b) praise for*

their mental

powers Whereas
intelligent

ones become

*c) most satisfied*

for their self–
unsuspecting

beauty Those
well–sourced

in both become


*d) suspicious*

of undue praise
of any kind

whereas ugly un
intelligent wo

men remain as


*e) wall flower*

s shut-off
from the most

necessary sun–
light apprais

als.

## Dandelion *(4)*

*a) s He a most*

intellectual

ly-sourced
English profess


*b) or once confid*

ed to me his

favorite flower
since childhood

remained the dandel
ion Many would


*c) find such taste*

"common" in the

sense of lower-
levelled but e

ven the so wide
ly spread field

*d) s of dandelion*

s remained un

impressed by
such unnecessary

additional come-
ons.


## Group flower *(4)*

*a) s in a common*

but representa

tional vase
and individ


*b) ually express*

ive ones re

mind me of
two types of

persons those

*c) needing that*

protective
group-feel

ing and o
thers often


*d) on their own*

blooming an

aura of orig
inal selfful

ness.


## *A window sill* (5)

*a) remains for my*

taste at least

as an ideal
place for still–

*b) lifes but such*

places usually

remain over-
filled with left-

overs from the


*c) living-room'*

s perhaps bet
ter situated

for social
time-telling


*d) s Still life'*

s require light

and additional
breathing space

*e) to enliven their*

most necessary

personal dialogu
ing opportun

itie
s.


## *That lengthen (2)*

*a) ing afternoon*

sleep represent

s its own self-
defining interest

s while keep
ing me from the


*b) genuinely mid-*

day sun-light

benefits and a
nother perspect

ive of poetic
self-finding

s.

## Milkweed those

free-flyers
blessing this

May's 3 o'clock
sunshine-appear

ances with a
singular voice

lightly express
ive of self-

reviving solo-
instinct

s.


## Erna Ernest (3)

*a) Weill's sculpt*

urally adept

wife became so
attuned to her


*b) down-staired*

workroom that

she neglected
her most sensi

tive husband'

*c) s needs for a*

life-engaging
togetherness

callings So he
upstaired his

ways otherwise.


## *Their piano (2)*

*a) top's become*

so congested

with varied
unrelated bric-

a-brac that
it's no wonder


*b) the difficulty*

it's encounter

ed in articulat
ing its own

individual
voice.

## If even *(4)*

*a) good modern*

poetry will

still communi
cate its own


*b) special voice*

then late Celan'

s very private
symbolic imag

ery and the


*c) late Tang's*

Li Shangyin
's so called

"hermetic

*d) poems" have creat*

ed their own
criteria for

such an under
standing.


## *Predicting (2)*

*a) the future We'*

re unable to

predict the
future because

the past and
present remain


*b) elusively mani*

fold–interpret

ed and because
the future fu

tures us
and not we

it.

## Window-in

or window-out
the window'

s become but
a transpar

ent alternate
route from

a static time-
telling only–

here and only–
now.


## Are those en (2)

*a) abled to in*

tegrate dog and

cat into a
familied unity

also seeking–
out a better


*b) means of rede*

signing their

own not so
certained

marital identi
ty–cause.

## Only love

can help over
come those

still fester
ing wound

s of a pre
vious street-

dog-like ex
istence.


## It's not "the (4)

a) best" who sur

vive (as if

we could ac
cept what "the


b) best" actually

means) most

usually defin
ed in our

mirroring
most-person

*c) al-way Perhap*

s it become

s easier to
realise why

the "unbest"
(each in a


*d) most personal*

way) have not

been routed
through time'

s most danger
ous pit-fall

s.


## Week-end mar *(8)*

*a) riages most*

always out of

occupation
al necessit

*b) ies perhaps*

remain most

vulnerable
because hus

band and wife


*c) have become*

daily otherwise-
tracked to se

parate–person
al–routine


*d) s Yet they be*

come particular

ly advantaged
sharing in re

trospect such

*e) diversified*

experience
s Israel as–

one–says has
rarely been en


*f) abled to chose*

its friends

But while it'
s inhabited

by all kind


*g) s of not*

only Jews
from over 100

countries it
remains recept

ive not only

*h) historical*

ly-linguistic
ly to a broad

range of ex
ceptional–dia

logue
s.


## *In a nation* (4)

*a) such as Germany*

where friend

ships have be
come mainly es


*b) tablished in*

their earlier

or even later
school-days

It becomes es
pecially diffi

*c) cult in our a*

ging years to

scent-out possi
ble future friend

s also because
we're both high


*d) ly-selective*

with our own

particular
sense-of-

choice.


## My father (10)

*a) most always*

(at least

theoreti
cally guid

*b) ed) by a*

liberal–pro

gressive–sense–
of–life always

maintained


*c) that we learn*

the most from
persons who see

and think o
therwise than


*d) ourselves*

through their

varied back
grounds Yet all

of his self–

*e) chosen partner*

s business
and otherwise

friends and ac
quaintance


*f) s were upper-*

middle-class

materialist
ic Jews my mo

ther's favor


*g) ite "variety'*

s the spice-
of-life prepar

ed the usual
weekly routine

*h) of Hamburger'*

s Monday Lamb

chop's Tuesday
Livered Wednes

day … …


*i) and until her*

mid–80s felt
that pepper

and otherwise
such spices


*j) remain out-*

of–bounds

classified
as "unheal

thy".

## Classifying *(4)*

*a) birds on the*

basis of size

color habitat
and the like


*b) misses their*

so poetic high–

flying sense
Those most al

ways on–the–
rush as house


*c) wife's expect*

ing visitor

s Those who
circle their

own singular
sense of spac


*d) iously sound*

less untouch

able realms and
those ground–

based worm–de
ciphering

… …

## A damp-down-(3)

*a) day motionless*

ly self-inhab

iting the quiet
of reflective


*b) time-pauses*

but neverthe

less listening
wide and depth

ed awake to the


*c) slightest of*

changeable
self-certain

ing colored-per
spective

s.

## *Do these* (2)

*a) hand-picked*

flowers real

ise perhap
s on a shady

spring day


*b) the intense*

coloring
s of their

pre-formed i
dentity-

cause.

*These time-* *(2)*

*a) extending*

fields now

growthed even
beyond the

scope of my
eye-awared


*b) landscaping*

s with spring'

s recurrent
life-prevad

ing timely-im
pulsing

s.

## Should we (3)

a) *distinguish*

between upper

and lower-lev
el Christian

s The one be


b) *ing more edu*

cated and cul
tivating a

more differen
tiated under

stand of God'


c) *s word If so*

we should real
ise Jesus chose

only lower-lev
el ones as

His disciple
s.

## Is genuine *(6)*

*a) country music*

the authentic

voice or e
ven soul of

*b) the common*

people To

judge that
we must know

who are the

*c) "common peo*

ple" and what
country music'

s genuine and
what's imitative

*d) Starting with*

Herder and Haydn

such music o
pened the way

to a trans


*e) national music*

al-sense but
such "folk"

music became
in time part


*f) and parcel of*

a national e

ven national
istic musical-

identity.

## *A single (2)*

*a) cricket seem*

s to have re

mained in our
long vacated

apartment
cricketing-


*b) out his domes*

tically occupy

ing one-toned
but invisibly

contemplat
ive where-a

bout
s.

## In the distan (3)

a) *ce white puffy*

clouds as young

children call
ed for a some


b) *what purposing-*

response Or

were they my
future poem

s not yet


c) *word-shaped*

for their new
ly formed–ex

pressive
ness.

## It's still

much-too-early
for the autum

nal fruit to
form where

the white bud
s now seem

to be herald
ing their fu

ture time-ful
filling cause.


## This fully (2)

*a) self-occupy*

ing mid-spring

afternoon
can best be

described
as stately


*b) vertically*

formed up-

standing
while most-

evidently
self-reassur

ing.

## Newly blown- *(2)*

*a) clouds being*

ushered-in

to take their
pre-ordain

ed if trans
itory-presen


*b) ce until*

these spring

winds have
arranged for

a complete
change-of-

scene.

## My retarded (4)

*a) son Raphael*

as helpless

as myself in
practical

*b) things Watch*

ing him try

to enter a
newly bought

beach chair

*c) from every*

possible dir
ection and

subordinate
eye-length

*d) s I could only*

admire Rosemar

ie for taking-
care-of-us-

both.

## Why become a (4)

*a) poetic state-*

official in

ancient Tang
China when

*b) poets should*

be attuned to

the truth and
not to their

expected court
ly flattery

*c) They mostly*

passed that
difficult and

comprehen
sive exam but

most-all soon

*d) lost their*

position
s as would be

expected of a
genuine open-

mouthed poet.

## Each of us (6)

### a) is endowed with

a right of

self-defense
these day


### b) s not with

sharp-edged

weapons but
with a self-

protective


### c) word-length

Few accept
personal

criticism
even if justi

*d) fied but the*

best means of

self-defense
remains a

willingness


*e) to hear what'*

s possibly in-
part-true or

better-yet
a developed

sense of self-


*f) irony that*

mutes critic
ism even be

fore it's
openly self-

articulated.

## It may have *(3)*

*a) rained the night*

through though

my dreams re
mained untouch

*b) ed by such*

nightly shadow

ings They pre
sented a mess

age of their
own which al

*c) most went un*

heard because

I slept my own
dreams elusive-

retimed other
wise-telling

s.

## Slides *(4)*

*a) The element*

ary school's

play-ground
sliding him


*b) down through*

pages of still

unwritten his
tory while the

time-lengthen


*c) ing one in Ill*

mensee entered
the arriving

waters with


*d) such a splash*

of vastly un
recorded cool

ing-off conver
sation

s.

## Taking espec (6)

*a) ial care of*

the diminish

ing bird popu
lation manifest


*b) ed here through*

feeding-boxes

I saw only
his tail hang

ing out of


*c) one of those*

bird-feeding
places perhap

s because the
over-sized ra

*d) vens had stol*

en all of his

tree-bottomed
reserved wal

nuts And then
those carefully


*e) made bird hou*

ses mirroring

perhaps the
taste of

their maker
s but not as


*f) it seems of*

the more dis

criminating
bird's own

nest-bound
home-feeling

s.

## He a once (10)

*a) reliable left*

fielder now

becoming with
age a butter-

*b) fingered in*

ept holder-

ons And then
writing down

other words
than he actual

*c) ly intended*

Good that he

keeps re-read
ing as a mean

s of self-de
fense

*d) A common*

history
creates identi

ty more than
just structur


*e) al and politi*

cal change

Good wishes to
all European

s although per


*f) sonally I hav'*

nt ever met
a single one

They're still
French German


*g) Italians A*

common history

has made them
what they are

Eastern Germany

*h) 's an import*

ant example of
this They re

main after de
cades of reuni


*i) fication closer*

in so many way

s to other
once Communist

ic East Europ
ean states


*j) than to Germany*

They can best

be described
as possible

late-starter
s.

*For some it* (4)

   *a) may be blood*

   that runs deep

   est through
   family-sponsor

   *b) ed veins But*

   for me it re

   mains person
   al religious-

   cultural attach
   ment One used

   *c) to call that*

   something like

   soul-length
   Call it what

   one will such
   friendship

*d) s for me cur*

rented with
what's deeper

and more last
ing than fam

ily-attachment.


## Chung our *(2)*

*a) dear Vietnam*

ese friend

says birthday
s are celebrat

ed there for
the mother who


*b) birthed from*

the depth of

her womb not
for the unre

membering
child.

*The best of (4)*

*a) early-age child*

ren's books

are those which
dialogue a

*b) complementary*

sense of equal

wave-lengths
between author

and artist Inter

*c) esting to know*

that many of
classical Chin

ese artists

*d) poetised what*

they painted
while painting

what they poet
ised.

## After wearing (4)

*a) a protective*

mask day-in

day-out one
begins to feel

*b) as if that*

mask had be

come a part
of one's own

person perhap

*c) s not as a*

masked gang
ster but more

like one of

*d) the Greek chor*

us with that
Sophoclean

tragic-feel
ing.

*These specially* (4)

  *a) Bavarian*

  "ice-saints"

  who appear year
  ly after some

  thing like a


  *b) May heat-swell*

  transforming
  the pre-summer

  weather back


  *c) to a winter'*

  s chill Frankly
  I'd prefer the

  correctly sain
  ted-ones with


  *d) their somewhat*

  more engaging

  miraculous-
  work

  s.

## Fluttering *(7)*

*a) s I'm perhap*

s an unre

liable wit
ness half-

*b) blind and e*

ven more-so

deaf but that
over-sized ra

ven just land

*c) ing toward*

s the top of
the hightest vis

ible tree hasn'
t stopped flutt

*d) ering its ex*

tended wing

s He doesn't
seem to be

mating – no o

*e) ther bird in*

sight nor eat
ing He's not

washing his
feathers either


*f) without a wa*

tering place

Why then the
almost uncon

trollable wing–


*g) fluttering-ex*

citement that
I begin to

feel like flut
tering therea

bouts as well.

## By mid-May (10)

*a) our world'*

s become so

fully flower
ed with con

trasting col


*b) ors shapes and*

luscious
scents that e

ven the invis
ible Corona

seems but re


*c) motely present*

hardly limit
ing nature's

out-spreading
beautifying–

*d) impression*

s Whatever

comes whether
wars plagues

natural dis


*e) asters even*

after the
heaviest of

losses life
continues on


*f) protected as*

The Good Lord

insists The
Great Bard

realised the


*g) tragic depth*

of man's exis
tence but al

ways at the
not-end even

*h) with the stage*

strewn with

corpses Life
continued on

a new order


*i) will be creat*

ed Death's

triumph how
ever great

always remain


*j) ed limited The*

Good Lord of
life remains

our resurrect
ed-sovercign.

## These newly (4)

### a) growthed leave

s now heavy

with rain e
ven I could

feel through


### b) my window'

s inspoken si
lences the

weight of
their timely-


### c) exposure

s When word

s become
weighted too

they should
learn in time

*d) the length and*

depth of their

appropriate
newly as

signed–express
iveness.


## *It had been* (4)

*a) afterall a long*

drive one of

many of their
life's recept

ive time–tell
ings yet some


*b) thing there*

where they'd

vacationed
on and off

for almost a
half–century

he sensed was

*c) missing At*

first it did
n't reveal

why until at
the waterfront

he realised
that somewhat


*d) shaky wooden*

pier had been

removed leav
ing but an ex

tending naked–
feeling far–

out–to–sea.

## Clues *(6)*

*a) As an obser*

vant poet he'
s become awared

of those per


*b) haps little*

things that
might reveal

something of
the other hotel


*c) guest's raison*

d'être For ex

ample why those
now cancer–af

fected Belgium

*d) s contined to*

breakfast alone
inside Why some

feed the ever-
persistant spar


*e) rows while o*

thers quick to

cover their
plated in self-

protection Minor


*f) clues but if*

correctly per
spectived major

indicators of
this or that.

## *Perhaps* (7)

*a) one of the*

most import

ant function
s of a ser

*b) ious poet is*

to enable his

reader's better
understand

ing of what

*c) makes their*

daily alarm
clock's self–

perpetuating

*d) ticking-away*

those second
s of an irre

trievable–
past Plays

*e) within a play'*

s not only a

Shakespear
ean even Piran

dello special


*f) ity but a*

mirroring of
our own life'

s dialogue
between what


*g) appears and*

who or what's

behind that
self-decept

ive appear
ance.

## Worry bird (4)

*a) s those on my*

mother's side

small town
Polish ghetto'


*b) s fly-away*

s from what

became actual
ly death-in

habiting


*c) If "there's*

nothing more
to fear than

fear itself"
Still those


*d) endemic fear*

s remained

time-telling
habitual-warn

ings.

## Corona in (3)

*a) its own way'*

s created a
one-world a

genda None of
the previous


*b) great empire*

s whether Greek
Roman Chinese

Spanish or
British could

feel so self–


*c) assured that*

their very-pre
sence remained

treated with
the greatest

of respect.

## It's hard-to- *(3)*

*a) say if your*

beloved life–
partner's dy
ing whether


*b) you feel more*

for him or
your own iden

tity–loss Such
a divided sen


*c) sibility can*

hardly flour

ish once a
gain on its

own well–de
served merit

s.

## Identity chains (5)

### a) Promiscuous

and prostitut
ed women must

learn to live


### b) with a bodi

less sense
of self-i

dentity The
silence after


### c) rain sounds

so thorough

ly as your
oft self-con

cealing iden

*d) tity-claim*

s You can
write your

fears off
but you may


*e) at least*

learn to re

veal their
own purpos

ing identity–
claim

s.

## *There remain* (3)

*a) many moment*

s of life-re

lief especial
ly when you


*b) or your dear*

one's "it's
not cancer"

as if life
itself's been


*c) reborn to your*

own need for
living-it-out

to its last
ing-extent.

## For those *(3)*

*a) curious-mind*

ed it's hard

to keep-out
of other peo

*b) ple's business*

easily reali

sing it's non-
of-your-own

however deeply

*c) you delve in*

to the unrhy
med here and

possible
their

s.

## *Are these* (3)

*a) trees and flow*

ers and the

welcoming
voices of spring


*b) walking through*

my leaving be

hind their
wind-reviving

impression


*c) s or have I*

walked them in
to my mind-in

voking time-
sensing

s.

## "He's not him (3)

a) self" she said

I responded

"What self has
he become"


b) She didn't ans

wer that one

either because
she didn't know

whether he'd be
come less of


c) his former self

or taken-on

a new sense of
self-being

which she had
n't known be

fore.

## 3 Chinese Master (3)

*a) pieces Zhao Menj*

ian Orchid 13 c.

forgetting
the especial

Chinese symbol
ism Line and

space say–it–
all simply

poetically–
lyrical.


*b) Shen Zhou*

Poet on a Mount
ain Top 1497

How small he'
s become with

the trees reach
ing–out for

his time–ascend
ing appearan

ce.

*c) Yun Shouping*

Magnolia Peony
and Pine ca 1700

A bouquet of
self-extend

ing imperman
ency.


## *It rained*

through the
night but

scarcely touch
ed my dream

ed–appearan
ces moonless

yet waved–
through their

tideless a
wakening

s.

## Poetic Dream *(4)*

*a) ed-Phrasing*

s Another of

those dream
ed poetic-se


*b) quences I kept*

writing but
those sheeted

words wouldn'
t stay-put


*c) entangled in*

their own
word–sensed

phrasing
s When I a


*d) woke nothing*

left of that

dialogued–
sleepful

ness.

## Stamina (3)

*a) 's the best*

word for what

I'm experienc
ing now in my

*b) 82<sup>nd</sup> year not*

stamina but the

lack-of-it
easily tired

following
more the body'

*c) s desire for*

sleep and rest

than my usual
up-and-about

s creative-rest
lessness.

*That tradition* (3)

   *a) al body-mind-*

   soul biblical

   interrelation
   ship doesn't


   *b) seem to work*

   for me my ship

   continues drift
   ing its more

   or less bodi
   less course


   *c) word-inhabit*

   ing yet no

   longer secur
   ing its ground–

   base satisfact
   ions.

# Learning Anew *(3)*

*a) Still in my*

aging-years

learning a
new as for ex


*b) ample about*

those so Bavar

ian Ice-Saint
s How should a

New York Jew
acquire expert


*c) ise here until*

directly affect

ed with their
cold-enticing

time-spell
s.

## It takes (4)

a) *time and per*

haps effort

to accommodate
oneself to


b) *foreign-new*

landscaping

s Gauguin
needed due

time but the


c) *restless Van*

Gogh already
at work deci

phering what


d) *he envision*

ed with his
almost wild

ly-activat
ing brush-

stroke
s.

## Back-on-Course *(for Rosemarie (4)*

*a) and Gerty) If*

the therapist'
s aim's getting

*b) the patient*

back-on-course

but why had
that become a

dead-end street

*c) Perhaps some*

still unnamed
side-street

would perhaps

*d) s route him*

or her in to
a newly-per

spectived-be
ginning.

## *At our age* (3)

*a) a painless a*

wakening

could seem
thoroughly

*b) out-of-place*

Such a desir

ed–beginning
would reveal

in due time as

*c) wrongly-add*

ressed with a
timely "re

turn to the
original-sender".

## Can one call *(2)*

*a)that the in*

itial poetic–

impulse The
mother's sway

ing back and
forth with the


*b) baby slowly at*

tuned to that

rhythmic repeti
tively samed

sleep's enchant
ed–quietude

s.

## Two way (4)

a) s If there'

s a right way

and an untouch
able wrong–


b) way She's most

intimately in

itiated since
childhood with

the way she'


c) s been taught

It's like list
ening to Chopin

for all the mis
takes his mo

ther once made

*d) dissatisfied*

if they're not
attuned to those

imploring
fingers as

well.


## Sunday-perspect (5)

*a) ive Some church-*

goers have be

come attuned
to a Sunday-


*b) perspective es*

pecially list

ening for those
special Sunday

church bells

*c) resounding a*

come-on and
let's-go But

Corona has
for weeks-on–


*d) end upset that*

Sunday-perspect

ive and left
many of those

church-goers


*e) as if deprived*

of what they'
ve so long

taken-for-gran
ted.

## A nation which (5)

*a) bloody civil*

war seems now
hard–of–remem

*b) bering It's*

rarely been
so divided

as now and
that division'

*c) s not only a*

one–man's

guilt but on
both sides a

refusal to

*d) compromise*

denying even
basic freedom

s Remember
too France be


*e) fore the Nazis*

invaded "a

nation divided
in itself can

not stand".

## Church bell *(4)*

*a) s Do these church*

bells though e

qually resonat
ing become never

*b) theless other*

wise receptive

ly-heard Some
with an histori

ical sense per

*c) sonal or other*

wise religious
ly attuned to

Jesus' resurrect
ion while still

*d) others complain*

ing of those

bells intruding
into their self–

withholding pri
vate sphere

s.

## *These 1938* *(2)*

*a) stars seem to*

be climbing–

me–up through
a dangerous

historical
domain I don'

*b) t look back*

but continue

on in to the
light of now

here's the pre
sent time–

hold.

## Should I *(4)*

*a) really prefer*

these richly-

sourced green-
time sameness–


*b) trees landscap*

ing a continu

ity of spring
ly fashioned-

designs or


*c) when they're*

nakedly on dis
play transform

ed through
their individ


*d) ually-reveal*

ing upstanding

otherwise
character-

trait
s.

## Church tradit (4)

*a) ions shouldn't*

be looked down-

upon They offer
us their own


*b) timely secur*

ing-rhythms

They guarantee
a yearly re

petitive same


*c) ness one might*

say in the
footsteps of

Christ In a
world where


*d) anything goes*

such tradition

s may reinhabit
a much-need

ed social-whole
someness.

## *Priorit* (9)

*a) ies and Per*

spective

s Two cent

*b) ral question*

s especial
ly for the

aging Which
have become

*c) your priori*

ties and have

you learned
to understand

anew through

*d) an otherwise*

but equally
realistic per

spective My
prioritie


*e) s have remain*

ed love (Christ

and Rosemarie)
that daily dia

logue we call


*f) "poem" and*

then friends
family and

culture All
else remains

*g) secondary*

While I've

learned that
experience

s (truth) re


*h) mains many-*

sided and I'

ve learned
in time which


*i) one(s) are*

most express

ive of my own
raison d'ê

tre.

## Even silenc (6)

a) *es (if listen*

ing in most
carefully)

retain their


b) *own individ*

ual lengths
depths and

shadowing
s Silence is


c) *where we've*

learned to re

ceive our own
receptive

voice however

*d) changeable*

In music it'
s what's heard

after sound
has relinguish


*e) its primpary*

expressive

ness It's that
after–rain


*f) feeling Silence*

remains the

most compell
ing of unheard

experience
s.

## Self revealing (4)

*a) She after over*

hearing a con

versation with
my son explain

*b) "what more*

will you have"

as that even
more than

Christian-to

*c) getherness*

enabling me
to rethink

what has real
ly never been

*d) static but*

growthed to

what should be
come a self-re

vealing father-
son relation.

## A good narra (2)

*a) tive poem should*

enable the act

ive reader to
fill-in all

those necess


*b) ary but untold*

empty-space
s It become

s more like a
Chekovian

open-ending.

## Self-protect *(2)*

*a) ive women have*

learned not to
play-all-their-

cards-out leav
ing the pre-


*b) designed act*

ive suitor

much that has
remained gen

uinely-un
touchable.

## Charles you *(6)*

*a) may be long*

dead though

you're still
hanging on our


*b) dining room'*

s wall 3 or

4 of your
best painting

s They're still
alive to your


*c) brush and tem*

pered feeling

s You've re
leased them

long ago but
they haven't

*d) released you*

from our most

personalis
ed remembran

ces If as she


*e) said "David'*

s poems are bet

ter than him"
then let them


*f) be read book*

by book des
pite my ever–

present help
ful–guidance.

## *That hasty (2)*

*a) on-the-way-to-*

work kiss has

become as an
ever–reworded

cliché left be
hind without


*b) genuine feel*

ings sensual

or not as a
not–so–spec

ial delivery-
postage.

## Only in re *(3)*

*a) trospect did*

the German capit

ulation in 1945
awaken a sense

of being freed


*b) (if at all*

from the habit
ual bombing

s) Rather it
acknowledged

a bitter de


*c) feat of an*

arrogant Sat
anically-en

thused self-
destructive

people.

# *Philosophi (2)*

*a) cal ideas only*

tangent the

upper shelve
s of our most

personal identi
ty-cause where


*b) as good poetry*

should remain

situated from
head-to-toe

completely
self-inhabit

ing.

## *Lutheran* (4)

*a) theologian*

s in general

have taken
themselve

*b) s far-too-*

seriously es

pecially when
one realise

s as a good

*c) Lutheran*

that The Good
Lord's good-do

ings remain perpet

*d) uated outside*

our own so
theological

ly self-import
ancy extra-nos.

## If life's a (5)

*a) continual pro*

cess of change

are we then
as those late

*b) 19<sup>th</sup> century*

Japanese wood

cuts the play-
thing of the

tidal force of

*c) those overdwell*

ing waves Or
do we have

some say in
the becoming

*d) of what and*

whom we'll be

come in time
and/or are

we continual


*e) ly pre-formed*

until that
gravestone

finalises us
in its own

lasting self-
image.

*For Reiner and* (2)

*a) Gerty The inter*

play of two

generation
s of two time'

s experience
perspective


*b) s a time-say*

of over–lapp

ing but still
on–going there

but only then–
as–now.

## If I'm sick (2)

*a) and suffering*

does that change

the landscaping
of what I've

continually
been seeing and


*b) if so is it*

because that

dialogued–land
scaping sympa

thises with my
own state-of–

being.

# Most mission *(2)*

*a) aries among o*

thers are marr

ied to a cause
I'm married to

a person Life


*b) for me's the*

cause itself
and love at

the center of
its daily be

ing-reactivat
ed.

## Where's the *(3)*

*a) border-line*

between self–

indulgence
and poetic ex

*b) pressive*

ness most al

ways in the
exacting choice

of words they'

*c) re there to*

help dialogue
the poem's

self–certain
ty.

## If we're hon (5)

*a) est with our*

selve we're

different with
each and every

*b) friend Which*

is the real

self in that
changing kalei

doscope of

*c) every otherwise*

I am I was a
dialogue that

ultimately
denies a "real

*d) self" What is*

normal Is it

a personal
way of balan

cing the-other-
side of an e


*e) lusive-change*

able-self Or

is it an ab
stract ideal

of efficient
ly working


*d) and loving*

Normal must

somehow in
habit us with a

sense-of
familiar

ity.

## Two ways (6)

*a) for Gerty The*

identity-con

flict of the
new Moslem mi

*b) grants between*

a tradition

al religious–
family-orienta

tion and the

*c) freedom espec*

ially for wo
men over mind

and body Do
the tradition

alists really

*d) live a caged-*

in-existance
or does that

familiar fam
ily-religious

culture provide


*e) a protective*

shield again
st foreign in

fluences Each
must decide

especially


*f) if they expect*

from themselve
s a newly ac

quired freedom-
of-choice.

## Numbers (6)

*a) 466 maybe for*

most just a
number but it

means for me
Mozart's great


*b) D Minor Piano*

Concerto Youth

s proudly sport
the number and

name of their


*c) soccer hero*

That number has
or will in

time become
an existen

*d) cial part of*

their very-be

ing I've alway
s lived ever-

since-child


*e) hood with the*

street number
22 now 13 plus

9 It seems that
I'm following


*f) my mother's*

example 22 has

come to mean
for me home-

base.

## A Sermon on (4)

*a) the Lord's pray*

er She preached

what she gen
uinely exper

*b) iences women'*

s domesticat

ed talk of
cleaning-up

in this case
her room (the

*c) proper place*

for prayer)

I came home
not having

been exposed
to a lofty bibli

*d) cal message but*

with the need

to clean-up
my oft disorder

ed room-span.

## Flimsy half-

spoken cloud
s on heaven

ly display
wind-direct

ioned but no
wheres else

to dissolve
into a time

less invisi
ble void.


## Witness (2)

*a) ing the bee*

fully poised

on that flo
wer's femin

ine receptiv


*b) ity sucking-*

out all that
sweetness

for his mascu
line pleasur

ed-desiring
s.

# Tracing those *(3)*

*a) pictures back*

through the

years he found
it difficult


*b) realising*

when and why

he could no
longer recog

nise himself


*c) even less so*

feeling into
the depths of

that other-
side-of-self.

## *If they've (3)*

*a) become unable*

to secure

ground-
base

wandering a


*b) bout as if*

dazed by un
told happen

ings and once
they've become

affected by


*c) untimely swoon*

ing the dialog
ue becomes se

curely-certain
ed "love-

sick".

## Each new *(3)*

*a) day brings with*

it a special

and personal
message It


*b) only become*

s dialogued

if you're
prepared to

listen to
it on its


*c) own term*

s timely dis

closing its
untouchable-

expressive
ness.

## Can the poet (2)

a) *ic voice also*

become trans

formed into
a didactive

teacherly


b) *one only if it*

purposes a
personal

ally recogni
sable word–

sense.

## "Diakonie" *(for Reiner) (4)*

*a) only become*

s personal
ly faced as


*b) in the medie*

val cloister
Cluny when

that face
filled with


*c) pain suffer*

ing hunger

poverty and
need became

transform


*d) ed into the*

features of
Christ's most

personal
ly expectant–

one.

## Small talk (4)

*a) of chatterly*

women over a

Robert Frost–
like fence


*b) only takes-*

on flesh and

blood when the
D. H. Lawrence

gardener


*c) seduces her*

(Lady Chatter

ly) into
the phrased–

landscaping


*d) of his sens*

ually time–
urging–ex

pectancie
s.

# The poetic-i *(3)*

*a) magination*

can lead one

completely-
unprepared


*b) and seeming*

ly off-track

into the den
sities of new

surprising
and most un


*c) expectant*

regions of one

's own previous
ly-establish

ed self-cer
taincie

s.

## Let's not mor *(3)*

*a) alise about*

Harvey W and

the others
for the high

*b) er they climb*

ed the more

devastating
that fall in

to previous

*c) ly unexplor*

ed regions of
imprison

ed "me-too"
feed–back

s.

## "Beware the be (4)

a) ginnings" like

red flag

s of an on
coming storm


b) when the plea

sure boats

should immed
iately return-

to-shore But


c) it seems that

China America
and Germany a

mong other
s ignored the


d) first sign

s of Corona'

s devastat
ing-beginn

ings.

## 2*nd* Commandment *(Moses) (12)*

*a) It seems that*

despite Jesus'

confrontat


*b) ion with Satan*

many of us
find it diffi

cult to accept
his personal


*c) existence*

The Manichees

realising the
full-existent of

evil in this

*d) world that*

Satan must be
uncreated

and an equal
rival of God


*e) Many higher-*

classed Jews
as Martin Buber

felt that evil


*f) was nothing*

more than an
absence of the

good even some
important

*g) Christian*

theologian

s have accept
ed this and

finally it's


*h) become quite*

common to
see the invis

ible Satan be
ing turned in


*i) to the im*

pressively

dressed and
personed Devil

thereby making

*j) him vulnerable*

to death's
claims What's

visible can
also be destroy

*k) ed by us Perhap*

s we should

simply learn
to accept the

*l) bible at face*

value even the

so important
2<sup>nd</sup> command

ment.

# Must poetry *(4)*

*a) always remain*

poetic I used

to think so
but now I real


*b) ise that what*

I have to say

as a cultural-
intellectual

historian isn'
t always poet


*c) ic Poetry also*

has change

able faces It
s very essence

remains absol
ute–compress

*d) ion and a*

choice of word

s that sustain
s its most–re

levant mean
ing.


# *Always be (2)*

*a) ware of beauti*

ful women's

twice–weaponed
with what sensi

tive men find
irrest

ibly


*b) fixating*

their flourish

ing smiles and
body's fully–

formed self–
creating tempta

tions.

## Left-behind (4)

*a) The gestapo*

crashed-in

their estate'
s front door


*b) while they*

were taking

the back-door'
s escape-route

as they fled


*c) to safety but*

she (my mother'
s new friend)

left behind
many thing

s but most


*d) valuable*

the language
of her self–

finding iden
tity-cause.

## Giving-one' (4)

*a) s-all It's*

hard to hold-

back if you'
ve much-to-


*b) give as our*

grandson Aron

talented but
accident-prone

a future ath


*c) letic teacher*

In sports one
must give-one'

s-all even if


*d) that "all" be*

comes called-
upon to its

very break
ing-point.

## The scent

of freshly-
cut-grass

greens my lei
sured mid–May

time with the
wind's ever-in

creasing invis
ibly sensed-

imagining
s.


## Corona (2)

*a) has created*

a conflict

between health-
measures and

personal freed


*b) oms and yet*

she continue
s to behave

in a blithe
ly unconcern

ed-manner.

## Attunement *(8)*

*a) s Have the*

Chinese with

their quarter-
tone-melodie

*b) s hatched do*

mestic bird

s attuned
for our ear

s to such

*c) hardly sing*

able even
hearable in

tonation
s My father

*d) perhaps to*

slow his own

pace down
referred quite

often to run-


*e) away-horse*

s which he
himself re

mained until
his fateful


*f) stair-invok*

ing-fall The

darkly colored
paint of our

vintage-wood

*g) en-house of*

1938 has be
gun wearing

down from its
original in


*h) tent perhap*

s in attune

ment with our
own aging–ap

pearance.

## "Straight from *(3)*

### *a) the horses*

mouth" Not be

ing a horse-
back rider my

### *b) self it's diffi*

cult for me to

judge if horse
s can communi

cate so well
Frankly their

### *c) language and*

daily behavior

estranges my
own sense for

poetic-transpar
encie

s.

# Being the (7)

*a) youngest and*

most spoiled

child "blessed"
with two elder

*b) sisters I've*

always longed

for a compati
ble brother

who could share
my daily hope

*c) s and fears*

When Reiner

spoke with
tears in his

eyes of his
newly death-en

*d) compassing*

brother I felt

that loss not
only for him

but for my

*e) self as well*

Empathy's a
most important

gift not only
for a therapist


*f) à la Rogers*

but on a

daily basis
Those self-im

portant person
s as our curr


*g) ent president*

only capable

of emphasiz
ing with their

own experien
ces.

# Keeping fear (3)

*a) awaiting as*

that arrogant

bird–killing
tom cat at our

*b) doorstep*

s I felt for

days as if en
closed not as

with Corona

*c) of a very*

touchable
even hurt-de

signing ene
my.

## Signed-up *(4)*

*a) 16 months in*

advance for

our diamond
(60$^{th}$) wedd


*b) ing anniver*

sary I more-

than–felt that
similarity

with my moth


*c) er's shortly*

expectant 105$^{th}$
birthday But

those on her
table–list


*d) came instead*

to her but

shortly–spon
sored funer

al.

## *That riding-* *(4)*

*a) high feeling of*

Neil my since

3rd grade close-
friend as if


*b) horse-backed*

to a gallop

ing no pit-
falls ahead I

take each day


*c) as more than a*

daily-bread
gift of love

and the poetic-
word despite


*d) a wavering un*

balancing

but straight-
ahead time-

route.

## Marriage is *(3)*

*a) not an educat*

ional experien

ce or at least
it shouldn'

t be We do


*b) learn in marr*

iage as a form
of self-help

the otherwise
ness of our

wife or hus


*c) band and per*

haps somewhat
more of our

own kaleido
scopic change

ability.

# *The open-(7)*

*a) door policy*

means for me

here and now
in summerly


*b) mid-May a pro*

liferation

of bees yellow
jackets and o

ther sting–


*c) accessible*

intruder
s But it meant

for the mid–
19th century


*d) Japanese an*

alternate way–

of-life that
meant progress

a new technol

*e) ogy imperial*

expansion and
ultimately

their atomic–
bomb downfall


*f) But for me*

the most mean

ingful of open
doors Kafka's

ever-so-slight
ly one but o


*g) pen to the e*

ternal light

of the Good
Lord's unapproach

able-holiness.

## Cricketing *(4)*

*a) I don't know*

why the habit

ually repeti
tive cricket


*b) doesn't tire*

of his incess

ant cricket
ing Either

he's no ear
s or lacks a


*c) sound-proof*

defense like

persons habit
ually-sourced

with Trumpian
self-praise


*d) They must need*

it otherwise

they'd have
stopped their

form of crick
eting long ago.

## All the hors *(3)*

*a) es were in*

the pasture

eating to
their heart's

and stomach's


*b) content except*

that last one
different

ly colored
standing motion

lessly aside Was


*c) he sick Why so*

inactive as a
child born to

a contempla
tive-otherwise

ness.

## *Those lilie* (2)

*a) s-of-the-valley*

reminding al

ways of my mo
ther's wedding

pictures inno
cently singing


*b) an enchanted*

but no longer

available
song of once–

upon–a–time
her time

their time.

## When retired (3)

a) *every day's be*

come like Sun

day has lost
its special

b) *appeal it*

shouldn't be

come that way
in marriage

that distance

c) *s from its*

initial and
most personal–

together
ness.

## Polonius (4)

*a) Evil has re*

tained its fas

cination for
some like

*b) children*

playing with

fire and a
dults in their

own way doing

*c) much of the*

same kind of
thing Evil

creates its
deadly mean

*d) s of dialogue*

Keep that
fire at a dis

tance Let it
burn itself

out.

## Old lesson (3)

*a) s must be*

learned anew

because we'
ve not yet

grown into


*b) their repetit*

ive otherwise
ness Old peren

nials sprout–
outs of their

pre–determin


*c) ing color*

s and yet
they've become

suddenly a
wared newly–

sensed.

# *Even when (2)*

*a) the mid-after*

noon begins

to cast but
momentary

shadowing
s it's become

*b) like moods*

drifting a

way as well
from the swoll

en cloud's e
volving depth–

find
s.

## These summer- *(2)*

*a) time clouds*

have been mov

ing my thought
s away The in

visible wind


*b) s have taken*

charge and
I begin to

feel like a
light-bound

boat.

## If name-call

ing's at the
origin of

word-making
Luther Shakes

peare and
… have re

claimed an
archaic-trad

ition.


## It clouded o

ver in the
night as if

something
full-of-dark

ness need be
concealed

as we slept
our unknown

half-innoc
ent way

s.

## "A bird in (10)

*a) the hand's bett*

er than two-

in-the bush"
somewhat relat

*b) ed to "don'*

t count your chick

ens before they'
ve hatched"

Such a doubling

*c) of similar ex*

pressions indi
cates a preval

ent too opti
mistic attitude

*d) towards future*

claims Has that

become character
istic of many

American
s Corona virus

*e) taught us a*

new that life'

s not a contin
uously attaining

of future-claim


*f) s We remain de*

pendent not only
on plagues but

on wars and
natural unexpec


*g) ted disaster*

s The more man

becomes inde
pendent of The

Good Lord's
claims over

*h) life love and*

death the more

we should be
gin to realise

our very basic–
limitation

s The need


*i) to be taught*

anew should
better enable

us to read
the-signs-of–


*j) the-times*

through our

most-personal
existencial–

experience
s.

# In mid-air (3)

*a) A poem may*

redirection

itself in mid–
air as a pilot

his plane to


*b) a safer land*

ing-place
Poems often be

gin themselves
s with word

s thought


*c) s or impuls*

ings whose land
ing-rights

must first be
come fully-auth

enticised.

## These tree (4)

a) s have become

so fully green

ed a house to
house garden


b) to garden vis

ual privacy

attained with
out fences or

other artifi


c) cial boundary-

markers One al
most become

s that uneasy


d) feeling of be

ing lost from
the where-am-

I and in-what-
direction.

## The good doctor (3)

*a) diagnosed "you'*

re becoming all-

dried-out" and
yet I've alway

s watered my


*b) self at least*

as efficient
ly as person

ally hand-cut
flowers but

must gladly


*c) admit we've no*

vase here to
contain my most

personal thought-
expressive

ness.

*Our favored* (5)

    *a) Italian restau*

    rant now three-

    phased accord
    ing to Corona'


    *b) s tentative*

    extending–

    laws First
    take-out

    side umbrell


    *c) ared guarantee*

    s until new
    ly inaugurat

    ed open-house
    d All-of-which

*d) reminds me of*

Haydn's oft in
itial three-

movement symphon


*e) ies until final*

ly extended

to their fully
self-purpos

ings.

## Indian-giver *(7)*

> *a) s They used to*
> be called Indian-
> givers taking-
> back what they'

> *b) d original*
> ly given–away
> which seems
> best exempli
> fied by the

> *c) double-faced*
> dealings of
> most authori
> tarian re
> gimes as Hit

> *d) ler's occupat*
> ion of the
> Russian–certi
> fied Baltic state
> s I'll continual

*e) ly own what I'*

ve once–upon–a–
time given–away

because I'm the
stronger But

in the actual


*f) Indian case be*

cause I'm the
weaker-partner

Indian-giver
s know no o

ther rules


*g) than their-own*

which continual
ly applied to

America's take-
over of former

Indian land
s.

## First-timed (4)

*a) If carefully*

observed each

day here in
middle to late


*b) May brings*

forth new fully-

pfledged flower
ings appearing

in their best
original color


*c) ings as Sunday*

church-goer

s dressed in
their finest

Nothing self-
deceptive

*d) about this ex*

cept perhaps

in their other
wise somewhat

dulled–down
daily appearance

s.


## The clouds

umbrellared
him in to

the reflect
ive silence

s of a mid–
day awareness

of that assem
blage of oppor

tunely flower
ed–coloring

s.

## That image (3)

*a) kept return*

ing the rich

Warsaw Jew eat
ing alone in

*b) a plush restau*

rant during the

deportation
s I kept say

ing to myself
"you're not

*c) that rich Jew"*

while disturb

ing echoing-
back "You're

not David Jaff
in".

## These semi- *(2)*

*a) white clouds in*

volving evolv

ing into a
changeable

harmonical


*b) ly self-secur*

ing wholeness
reminding of

Victoria's
contrapunct

al fluenc
ies.

## It sometime (2)

*a) s matters the*

extent and di

versity of
one's cultural

vocabulary


*b) to realise*

what may seem
for others

as but obscure
ly footnoted–

reference
s.

*Are these* (3)

> *a) stream-lined*
>
> clouds to be
>
> recognized
> as a heaven

> *b) ly hymnal pro*
>
> cessional
>
> on display
> for all who
>
> feel moved by

> *c) their semi-re*
>
> ligiously ex
> pressive-
>
> raison d'ê
> tre.

## *Why do most* (2)

*a) trees find it*

necessary

to communicate
through their

outspreading
underground

*b) roots Would*

they feel en

dangered if that
message came–

out in to
the open–air.

## The poet (3)

a) *doesn't come*

first and

then the crit
ic As Warren


b) *wrote "We've*

been poemed"

(not poeted)
that means

both poet and


c) *critic Michel*

angelo's mar
ble had been

angelical
ly pre–concei

ved.

## From out of *(3)*

*a) my unremember*

ed past they

came non-qual
ity songs but

with a mess


*b) age for here*

and now So
at first I

began to lis
ten careful

ly but then be


*c) gan to sing*

along until
their message

had become a
part of my

present-day
me.

## Neil still re *(11)*

*a) members those*

5 girls including

my cousin Madel
ine he sent

*b) valentine*

cards to in

the 3rd grade
That's his

thing not mine

*c) My early child*

hood memories
remain large

ly diffuse as

*d) that Brigadoon*

town awakened
to life but

only every 100
years I can hard

*e) ly identify*

with those var

ied picture
s from my

youth The ear


*f) liest ones from*

age 2 or 3 al
most complete

ly interchange
able straight


*g) through to the*

fake-news of

my Bar Mitzvah
then the gawky

adolescent


*h) followed close*

ly upon the
(also) inter

changeable
scholar-learn

*i) er But then who*

ever could have

inhabited that
Jewish–Lutheran

minister The
poet–David seem


*j) s to have ta*

ken all these

by-paths to a
now still uni

dentifiable
self only


*k) through those*

pictures with

Rosemarie does
he discover his

identifiable-
self.

## An open-(2)

a) *air service*

for Ascension

Day as if
heaven and

earth but a


b) *time-place*

unity for
Christ's creat

ional word'
s expressive

ness.

## Those 5 (5)

a) *Walnuts The*

more he envis

ioned those 5
walnuts on his

b) *balcony as a*

self-perpetuat

ing still-life
The more they

kept answer

c) *ing-back as a*

phrased-unity
meant for pass

ing-by squirr
els or over-

*d) sized raven*

s to be open

ed from a
height of a

certifying–


*e) response But*

for now at
least our most

private dialogu
ing still–

life.

# Ascension Day (7)

*a) Is heaven a*

place or a

condition
or both As

*b) it's timeless*

it become

s impossible
for us here

on this chos

*c) en-planet to*

identify its
whereabout

s Is love
Christ's cruci

*d) fied love the*

pre-condition

for its very
existence

If so His

*e) faith and our*

s have become
timeless

as well But
let's never


*f) forget the*

close-logic

of our thought
s always re

mains on a


*g) far-lower-lev*

el than His
for us unimag

inable purpos
ings.

## In these Cor (4)

*a) ona times church*

services now

allowed as Greek
tragedies only


*b) with choric-*

masks and an

appropriate
distancing

No loud enthu
siastic sing


*c) ing allowed for*

fear of spread

ing germs Bett
er perhaps

as earlier
Christians or


*d) trees rooted*

(routed) in

a secretive
unsuspecting

underground-
depth.

## These cloud (5)

*a) s appear as if*

they have so

much to communi
cate yet upon


*b) 2<sup>nd</sup> thought*

they continue

on their un
chartered

way not real


*c) ising from*

where to what
wind–blown ap

pearance
s Clouds may

238

*d) have once receiv*

ed heavenly call

ings as with
Hennoch Elijah

and of course
Jesus But now


*e) they remain as*

dreams amorphous

ly floating a
bout for many

without rhyme
or reason.

## On Ghosts (3)

*a) He couldn't*

answer why

The Ghost of
Canterville


*b) was allotted*

300 years

whereas Jana
cek's 100 more

Ghosts seem to
be dead but a


*c) live enough*

to haunt their

victims while con
tinuing to breathe

in a phantom
ed-imagery.

# They say (2)

*a) "He gave in*

to himself"

If so who's
the giver and

who's the re
ceiver Had he


*b) become momen*

tarily two per

sons or is the
one more or

less two-faced
and/or one-

bodied.

## When confront *(4)*

*a) ed with death*

life itself

takes–on a
new–quality

*b) It become*

s once again

despite pain
s and fear

s freshly–sour

*c) ced first-tim*

ed as present
ly–neared as

death after

*d) Christ had*

crucified
its once–u

pon–a–time
calling

s.

## These muted (2)

*a) reflection*

s on the wall

remind of
once dream

ed–recurren
cies They rhy

*b) thm what's*

lost its pul

sed–urgency
and yet they

remain appar
ently soul

less–vacant.

## Just the two-

of–us silent
ly tabled to

the outside of
this late May'

s afternoon
ed time–tell

ing bright
nesses.

# My 4<sup>th</sup> edit (5)

*a) ion of Spanish*

literature

needing all
those extra

*b) editions to*

take-on recon

firmed prejud
ices against

Spain's so-

*c) called backward*

late medieval
culture its In

quisition
fanatic Cathol

*d) ic repression*

of Holland's
freedom-lov

ing people
s and their


*e) destruction*

of the Inca'

s highly develop
ed civilisat

ion.

## The world I (4)

*a) left behind be*

cause it wasn't

the place and pro
mise of what I've

*b) become and this*

impersonal

one that hasn'
t claimed me

yet as its

*c) own We've creat*

ed a world of
ours an is

land in the
midst of con

*d) flicting wave-*

lengths never

theless safe
and secure

timely–pre
sent.

## These bud (10)

*a) s have sudden*

ly bloomed in

to an unexpect
ed yet pre-or

dained self-


*b) sustaining*

coloring amass
ing that ever-

present I-told-
you-so look

somewhat like


*c) my aging poet*

ic response
to this newly-

discovered
creative

word-flow

*d) If it was*

all meant-to-

be-so and
yet I've play

ed my part
in opportune


*e) ly designing*

those now safe

ly-secured
poetic-call

ings The most


*f) prevasive*

of all creat
ive-dialogue

s Our lower-
level free-

will and that


*g) higher upstair*

s of The Good
Lord's pre-de

termining
commanding

*h) time-view*

Life's the ulti

mate biblical-
blessing even

the crucifix


*i) ion's spelling-*

out "the death
of death"'

s timely hold-


*j) on-us freed*

for the eter
nal reassuring–

resurrect
ion.

## Are Ideas of (4)

*a) Grandeur in*

herent in
America's

Manifest Des


*b) tiny Not an*

"Age of Inno
cence" but

a land-based
vocabulary


*c) of unlimited*

superlative-

scope Mark
Twain and Don

ald Trump have
language


*d) our really not*

so self-con

taining Idea
s of Grand

eur.

# The more I *(3)*

*a) look to see*

if those 5

balconied-
walnuts have


*b) been squirrel*

ed or bird–

taken the bigg
er they've

become Or is


*c) it the time-*

length of my
reconfirm

ing eye-fo
cus.

## For Matthew *(3)*

*a) A girlfriend*

or should we

call it girl
friend same


*b) word used for*

an otherwise

relationship
sailing its

pre-given
route with the


*c) ambigious*

flag(s) of that

otherwise
shared-desir

ings.

# When help' (4)

*a) s not wanted*

it's better

to retire to
one's own

*b) prayers and con*

templation

s Each of us
retains as he

himself the
right even of

*c) self-destruct*

ion Or must we

in God's name
intervene

Who are we
afterall to

*d) speak in God'*

s name but at

a hand's time-
withholding

length.

*"What would* (10)

> *a) you do in such*
> 
> a situation"
> 
> My father'
> s typical and

> *b) less than self-*
> 
> reliant way
> 
> of involving
> another for the
> 
> full–responsi
> bility He or

> *c) she (unlikely*
> 
> for him) could
> 
> best answer
> "Sir I'm much
> 
> obliged for
> your confiden

> *d) ce in my judg*
> 
> ment but it's
> 
> afterall your
> decision to–
> 
> be-made." My

*e) "liberal-mind*

ed" father

favored the
death-penalty

because of the


*f) money saved*

from the obli
gation of feed

ing and housing
that most delin


*g) quent unworthy*

prisoner Money-

minded remained
the name of

his so-called
liberality.

*h) There's so*

much cleaning–
up to be

done in my
own case that


*i) I do feel un*

easy especial

ly after Jesus
words about

judging some


*j) one else who'*

s perhaps bett
er and more

worthy even
willing to


*k) partnership*

a monied–good

works deal
with The Good

Lord Himself.

## Now that As (3)

*a) cension Day*

has passed

we can come
back-down to


*b) this good*

earth's betok

ening bene
volence through

a now possible
beer-garden'


*c) s engaging Bavar*

ian-style food

and a pond-en
circling self-

sufficient to
getherness.

## Those thin (4)

*a) and high-level*

trees a com

plete woods of
them at the

Deininger Wei
her left my


*b) eyes search*

ing for height

s beyond reach
of my down-

bred darken
ing quietude


*c) s Those dark*

ly sourced wa

ters time-tell
ing an invis

ible depth
that matched

*d) in its own*

way that pha

lanx of tree'
s inherent

growth-find
s.


## It's almost (2)

*a) always those*

pre-school child

ren from say
2 to 5 that

awaken an affin


*b) ity to my own*

(re)discovery
of a world

that's just
waiting to be

come known.

## Although (2)

*a) only shortly*

dead at a

ground–depth
of impenetra

ble silence
s Ingo still


*b) awakens in*

me a common

vocabulary
of biblical

ly-sourced
yet so actual

ising-truth
s.

# Instead of a (4)

*a) prelude my eyed-*

preception

s not yet sit
uating a sabb

*b) ath Saturday-*

feeling of a

concentrat
ed inspoken

ness Still a

*c) waiting the*

necessary
words to dis

tinguish the

*d) inherent vis*

ual realms of
this mid-air

ed feeling-
sense.

*Corot must* (6)

> *a) have chosen*

> his own allur

> ingly naked-
> model She

> *b) could feel*

> from the first

> his fully sens
> sed eyes land

> scaping her so

> *c) personally a*

> waiting his
> finely-touch

> ed brush–

*d) strokes avid*

ly availing
his completed-

thorough
ness Did she


*e) feel she'd*

been prostitu

ing her so
delicate

ly refined–
body and/or


*f) that she'd be*

come an intri

cate part of one
of France's most

poetically land
scaped–paint

ings.

## *I saw the* (7)

*a) consequence*

s of marrying

a beautiful
woman as my

*b) Aunt Sylvia*

had once ad

vised It was
on the boat

to Israel I

*c) was leading a*

group of my
own when an

attractive
young lady

*d) came up to*

me asking for

my protection
as she al

ready had

*e) attracted*

a crowd of
young men

swarming a
bout her as


*f) flies dis*

covering a

tasty left–
over meal

I took up


*g) the challenge*

especially
as her genuine

boyfriend was
an Israeli.

## Another one (4)

*a) of spring's en*

demic darkly a

massed shadow
ings not the


*b) kind of day*

for mood–domin

ating middle-
aged women

He a poet of


*c) mainly late-*

callings in
self-defense

preferred a


*d) dialogue with*

the fullest
of those new

ly colored–
blossoming

s.

*"Tongue-in-* (2)

a) *cheek"'s a*

hard one to

imitate al
though it say

s what it


b) *has-to-say*

in the most
picturesque

of English
self-inhabit

ings.

## Hopefully *(3)*

*a) "with no*

strings attach

ed" But what
would little


*b) children*

with their

heavenly-high
perhaps big

red balloon
hold–on–to


*c) without those*

strings attach

ed to their
fingering

such spacious–
imagining

s.

# How can you *(3)*

*a) serve a church*

that did little

to nothing to
help your own

*b) and God's own*

people survive

the barbaric
Holocaust

I'm not serv
ing that church

*c) but what could*

have been and

should have
been an ex

ample for the
future.

## To the memory (2)

*a) of Michael Butler*

You might call

them stranger
s intruder

s these mini-
clouds rushing


*b) by my extend*

ed length-of–

view I couldn'
t catch-up

until they be
came lost–

from-sight.

## Don't moral *(3)*

*a) ise Don't try*

to prove your
pointing fin

ger's longer


*b) and more effect*

ive even than
the Polonius-

type teacher
Rather learn

to mirror


*c) yourself in*

to what's
daily in need

of an effi
ciently recon

ciling self-i
mage.

## The only- *(2)*

*a) child years*

after my eld

er sisters had
left for coll

ege somehow a
bandoned to


*b) myself not*

knowing the

where or why
of things yet

significant
ly on–my–own.

## They may (3)

*a) have been*

familiar voic

es but they
neverthe

*b) less establish*

ed themselv

es daily as
first heard I

mean the deli
cate coloring

*c) range of spring*

flowers and the

unseen bird's
repetitive

ly voiced–en
semble

s.

# *Are these pass (4)*

*a) ing clouds sim*

ply on display

or are they
withholding

*b) a concealed*

message in an

indecipher
able language

of their own

*c) No art has e*

ver approached
the interwoven

complexity of

*d) such habitual*

ly harmonical
ly spaceful re

establishing–
design

s.

## The telephone *(3)*

*a) didn't ring at*

Chung's place

We feared for
the worst No

*b) means of con*

tact for us

Another of our
closest friend

s The list's

*c) getting smaller*

and smaller
Not even a

chance to say
goodby.

## As these (2)

*a) trees have been*

engaged for

centurie
s in under

ground conver
sations Have


*b) they been*

used for spy

ing on our
secret most

private even
political whis

pering
s.

## Man has at (4)

*a) least since*

the so-called

"Enlighten
ment" been in

*b) creasing his*

own self-im

portance while
becoming more

and more inde
pendent from

*c) his creator*

and Savior en

dangering e
ven destroying

the so-called
lower-level

*d) pre-human*

creation

s all in the
name of

progress.

## What's become ta (4)

*a) ken-for-granted*

when disallow

ed as during
the Corona


*b) crises sudden*

ly becomes most

necessary
in the name

of basic demo
cratic freed


*c) oms Crises of*

most any

kind can help
reestablish

what we've
most always


*d) taken-for-*

granted and

that's true
of marital–cri

ses as well.

## Surprising (4)

*a) and most plea*

sant as well

that our grand
children around


*b) 20 continue to*

vacation with

us as a family
at Whitsum

time while
Rosemarie and


*c) I could hard*

ly have wished

vacationing
with our so–

otherwise


*d) grandparent*

s But then
our together

ness mainly
reserved-for–

otherwise-
tasty-meal

s.

*I still remem (5)*

    *a) ber 2 minor in*

    cidents which

    increased my be
    lief in what'

    *b) s really import*

    ant and even

    known Rosemarie'
    s teacher dis

    playing a true

    *c) knowledge of*

    what I am and
    have become

    "That's the
    poet David Jaffin"

*d) and when our*

dear friend

Thomas Baumann
commented "you'

*e) ve taken such*

a personal

effort in cul
tivating your

friendship
s".

## If The Good (3)

*a) Lord's parti*

cularly near

those in
need is it be


*b) cause He experien*

ced that himself

and expects
that of his

followers and/
or because when


*c) we become help*

less the only

possible genuine
helpfulness

becomes most
necessary.

# The remember *(4)*

*a) ing images and/*

or experience

s we associate
with certain


*b) persons and/*

or places may

seem then as
now trivial

yet because
we remember


*c) means they*

have or alway

s were some
how of person

al importance
They land-


*d) mark on their*

own what we

didn't mark-
out for our

selve
s.

## Perhaps why (3)

   *a) philosopher*

s and psycholo

gists have al
ways remained

suspicious of


   *b) poets and poet*

ic truths not
only because

they're multi-
sensual but also

elusively not


   *c) fit for philo*

sophical or
psychologi

cal categorie
s they contin

ually deny.

## If we haven' (2)

*a) t achieved a true*

mastery over

our own
feelings then

temptation


*b) of that kind*

represent a
real undenia

ble and self–
encompass

ing actual
ity.

## Chung? *(3)*

   *a) Waiting for a*

   call that may

   never come
   It's not a

   death-senten


   *b) ce yet but his*

   person dead or
   alive has be

   come unreach
   able His phone'

   s no longer


   *c) in use and we'*

   ve no one we

   can turn to
   waiting for a

   call that may
   never come.

*Time may re (5)*

*a) main except at*

impossibly

high speed
s persistent


*b) ly unchange*

able and yet

we feel it
often other

wise Aging


*c) means that time'*

s speeding-up
day by day

year after year
as if being

*d) called to its*

final resolut

ion While look
ing back to


*e) our youthful*

days its seem

s as if mount
ained distant

ly-away.

# If you believe (2)

*a) as Neil that*

you're becom

ing younger-
stronger either

you're living
with an incur


*b) able case of*

an all-encom

passing wish
ful-think

ing But what
if it's act

ually true.

## I doubt (3)

*a) at times that*

the wind com

pared by Christ
ians to the


*b) Holy Spirit*

realises the

where and what
of its invis

ible being


*c) direction*

ed yes by an
unseen but irre

sistible
force.

## That continu *(3)*

*a) ous impulsing-*

to-write eith

er sourced by
the oncoming

*b) poem itself*

or through

my mind's
habitually

activating

*c) sense-for-mea*

ning but most
probably dia

logued by
both.

## *Is abstract* (5)

> *a) art a denial*
>
> of the unlimit
>
> ed beauty of
> The Good Lord'

> *b) s creation or*
>
> is it an accept
>
> ance of man's in
> ability to com
>
> pare with the

> *c) variety and*
>
> depth of na
>
> ture's all-in
> habiting per
>
> fection and/

*d) or an attempt*

to transfer

the artist's
most personal


*e) receptivity*

into limited

most subject
ive express

ive-form
s.

## Even shadow (4)

*a) ings possess*

a hardly lim

ited range of
density perhap

*b) s comparable*

to our wood'

s 3 depthed
greeness

es At the
nearest lower

*c) level a youth*

ful light

green middle-
ranged a fully-

sourced mature-
greenness and

*d) at the high*

est level dark

ening into its
death's alway

s present call
ings.

## The older we (7)

*a) become the more*

subjective

our sense for
the aging pro

*b) cess At time*

s a rather un

successful
imitation of

youthful vi

*c) gour "I'm not*

old you know"
from my 90-

year-old fa
ther At the o

d) *ther end a*

death-down

closeness to
death's motion

lessly adept–


e) *callings As a*

child the ag
ing appeared

to my unknow
ledgeable

future–sense


f) *as if inhabit*

ing a world
foreign to my

own sense of
life's very-be

ing Now picture


g) *s of my child*

hood days fail
to fully in

habit my
cultivating

word–sense.

## Are the in *(4)*

*a)terior private*

spheres of the

poet's life so-
called "confess

*b) ional poems"*

trivial by

their very na
ture or can

they open–up

*c) similar dimen*

sions of the
reader's own

experience

*d) s If so they*

may become
impersonal

ly–personal
ly relevant.

*Did I become* (5)

    *a) more-of-a-Christ*

    ian when christ

    ened as before
    when my faith


    *b) was founded*

    "only" through

    the bible church-
    going Jesus' God

    ly words His


    *c) crucifixion*

    and Resurrect
    ion Jesus' word

    s should never
    be relativised

*d) yet I've come*

to feel more

and more
as a minister

in a state–
church that


*e) christening*

s have become
little more

than a "holy
churches" name–

becoming re
levancy.

## Many of us (4)

a) *possess (or*

perhaps should

possess) an
untouchable

b) *that me-mine*

no intruder

s allowed

not even that
other-side-of–

c) *self If you*

fail to re
spect that

ultimate
reign-of-pri

d) *vacy you should*

be closed-out

most certain
ly for at

least a life–
sentence.

# I'm not to (4)

### a) blame sometime

s the pace

becomes too
fast for keep

### b) ing-up leav

ing behind

what should
have remained

indelibly fix
ated as Warren

### c) and Manfred Sie

bald's expert

evaluation
s The poem'

s responsible
not me it

### d) keeps to its

own ways as

each of us
soon to be

come blemish
ed-from-sight.

## "I can do (5)

*a) anything bett*

er than you"

a marriage and
friendship'


*b) s non-starter*

Those poised

at such height
s as that

aristocrat


*c) ic rider time-*

telling Maximil
ian's street

s once exalted
thorough-fare

*d) Take him down*

as a role-mo

del and become
endeared to

that part of


*e) your clumsy*

butter-fing
ered first-

class sloppi
nesses self.

## 3 close *(6)*

*a) friends lost*

within a short

time's bleed
ing somewhere


*b) s deep in my*

mind's soul

led for a per
sonal protect

ion against


*c) losses of this*

time–encompass
ing kind

self pity'
s among the

*d) lowest form*

s of empathy

And yet it
seeks inhabit

ing now 3


*e) friendship*

s each of which
sailing under

their self-ac


*f) comodating*

flagged and
dialogued

identity-
cause

s.

## May 26 Noth (2)

a) *ing new to be*

seen the early

morning sun
has already o

pened the blos
soming scent


b) *of a late*

spring day

colored in
its pre-chos

en most parti
cular identity-

source.

# *Still no (4)*

*a) word from or*

about Chung

as his phone'
s no longer

*b) in use we*

fear the same

of his person
as well I'll

miss most es

*c) pecially his*

finely-sensed
cultivated

understand

*d) ing of my*

better-self'
s poetic-ex

pressive
ness.

## *The closely-* *(7)*

*a) timed-loss of*

3 of my best

friends to
death's inhabit


*b) ing sameness*

abandoned

from my usual
ly unremember

ed dialogue


*c) Martin with*

his Schwabian-
bred sly-hu

mour Ingo
rhyming our


*d) often unrhym*

ed-together

ness Chung
what one-call

ed same

*e) or most simil*

arly-souled
now left to

our undivid


*f) ed past*

My flag re
mains lower

ed to half-
mast signify


*g) ing an unre*

deemable

most person
al-loss.

## Rediscover (5)

*a) ing Cherubini'*

s most origin

al Italian–
French contri


*b) bution to the*

Viennese classi

cal past Its
so different

iated express


*c) iveness whether*

in those seldom
heard 6 string

quartets or the
depthed relig

*d) iousity of those*

earlier masses

Something's miss
ing without

him despite the

.

*e) almost unlimit*

ed creative-im
pulsing of Haydn

Mozart and Beet
hoven.

## Can an artist (4)

*a) ic closeness*

to poets compos

ers and paint
ers long dead


*b) serve as an*

otherwise

kind of friend
ship replacing

the loss of


*c) one's personal*

once-alivened
friends And

then our love-
marriage con

tinues to pre-


*d) determine the*

length and
depth of

our most
loving-need

s.

## Is this the *(2)*

*a) end or the be*

ginning of a

book It actual
ly matters

little for
these poem


*b) s these book*

s remain as

a unity of
time's change

able express
ive needs.

## That poor (2)

*a) fly's no-ways-*

out climbing
up and down

the closed
door's window

ed-frame What


*b) does he real*

ly need either
here or there

imprisoned
in a slowly

dying life-
urge.

# Each morning (4)

*a) I wake-up as*

those post war–

time widows
with their hus

*b) bands listed*

as "missing in

action" and
Chung still miss

ing No concrete
proof of wheth

*c) er he's dead*

or alive though

most likely
dead How long

will this un
resolving ten

*d) sion remain*

for some of

those widows e
ven 3 or 4

years.

## The bushes (4)

*a) my bushes at*

the other end

of the garden
watered daily

*b) through that*

long dry-spell

now blooming
high and fully

flowered with

*c) their instinct*

ual coloring
s Water and

sun their life-
reclaiming

*d) source With me*

it's Rosemarie

and the ever-
present dialogu

ing word.

# Winds at the (2)

*a) unseen tower*

ing height of

this tree'
s green ex-

panse time-


*b) telling the*

heavenly blue'
s still un

spoken word-
expressive

ness.

## *Was Schütz des (2)*

*a) pite his Italian*

ate influence

s the most Pro
testant of com

posers the
first to intone


*b) biblical word*

s to their

lasting mean
ingful religious

and most per
sonal recalling

s.

## Compare Cherubi (12)

*a) ni's 5<sup>th</sup> Quartet*

especially

those last two
fully-depthed


*b) and unlimited*

ly resourced

movement
s with the

very best of


*c) the Viennese*

classical
masters and

if your listen
ing hard enough

*d) without Schumann*

esque reservat

ions you'll be
come transform

ed through


*e) little known*

and performed
music on the

very hightest-
level Schumann


*f) better known*

in his own

day as a mus
ic critic than

as a composer

*g) though emotion*

ally little-re
served in his

judgment
s reflecting


*h) often more of*

himself than

the composer
rescued Schu

bert more or


*i) less from obscur*

ity and intro
duced the very

young Brahms
as the new

*j) Beethoven*

High quality

yes but most
certainly not

Beethovian
But to relegate

the greatest


*k) of innovator*

s Haydn to
the ash can of

past master


*l) s and heard*

Cherubini
with a concen

trated ear
and a deaf

one as well.

*In Nomine Domini!*
*May 26 2020*

## Poetry books by David Jaffin

1. **Conformed to Stone,** Abelard-Schuman, New York 1968, London 1970.

2. **Emptied Spaces,** with an illustration by Jacques Lipschitz, Abelard-Schuman, London 1972.

3. **In the Glass of Winter,** Abelard-Schuman, London 1975, with an illustration by Mordechai Ardon.

4. **As One,** The Elizabeth Press, New Rochelle, N. Y. 1975.

5. **The Half of a Circle,** The Elizabeth Press, New Rochelle, N. Y. 1977.

6. **Space of,** The Elizabeth Press, New Rochelle, N. Y. 1978.

7. **Preceptions,** The Elizabeth Press, New Rochelle, N. Y. 1979.

8. **For the Finger's Want of Sound,** Shearsman Plymouth, England 1982.

9. **The Density for Color,** Shearsman Plymouth, England 1982.

10. **Selected Poems** with an illustration by Mordechai Ardon, English/Hebrew, Massada Publishers, Givatyim, Israel 1982.

11. **The Telling of Time,** Shearsman Books, Kentisbeare, England 2000 and Johannis, Lahr, Germany.

12. **That Sense for Meaning,** Shearsman Books, Kentisbeare, England 2001 and Johannis, Lahr, Germany.

13. **Into the timeless Deep,** Shearsman Books, Kentisbeare, England 2003 and Johannis, Lahr, Germany.

14. **A Birth in Seeing,** Shearsman Books, Exeter, England 2003 and Johannis, Lahr, Germany.

15. **Through Lost Silences,** Shearsman Books, Exeter, England 2003 and Johannis, Lahr, Germany.

16. **A voiced Awakening,** Shearsman Books, Exter, England 2004 and Johannis, Lahr, Germany.

17. **These Time-Shifting Thoughts**, Shearsman Books, Exeter, England 2005 and Johannis, Lahr, Germany.

18. **Intimacies of Sound,** Shearsman Books, Exeter, England 2005 and Johannis, Lahr, Germany.

19. **Dream Flow** with an illustration by Charles Seliger, Shearsman Books, Exeter, England 2006 and Johannis, Lahr, Germany.

20. **Sunstreams** with an illustration by Charles Seliger, Shearsman Books, Exeter, England 2007 and Johannis, Lahr, Germany.

21. **Thought Colors,** with an illustration by Charles Seliger, Shearsman Books, Exeter, England 2008 and Johannis, Lahr, Germany.

22. **Eye-Sensing,** Ahadada, Tokyo, Japan and Toronto, Canada 2008.

23. **Wind-phrasings,** with an illustration by Charles Seliger, Shearsman Books, Exeter, England 2009 and Johannis, Lahr, Germany.

24. **Time shadows,** with an illustration by Charles Seliger, Shearsman Books, Exeter, England 2009 and Johannis, Lahr, Germany.

25. **A World mapped-out,** with an illustration by Charles Seliger, Shearsman Books, Exeter, England 2010.

26. **Light Paths,** with an illustration by Charles Seliger, Shearsman Books, Exeter, England 2011 and Edition Wortschatz, Schwarzenfeld, Germany.

27. **Always Now,** with an illustration by Charles Seliger, Shearsman Books, Bristol, England 2012 and Edition Wortschatz, Schwarzenfeld, Germany.

28. **Labyrinthed,** with an illustration by Charles Seliger, Shearsman Books, Bristol, England 2012 and Edition Wortschatz, Schwarzenfeld, Germany.

29. **The Other Side of Self,** with an illustration by Charles Seliger, Shearsman Books, Bristol, England 2012 and Edition Wortschatz, Schwarzenfeld, Germany.

30. **Light Sources,** with an illustration by Charles Seliger, Shearsman Books, Bristol, England 2013 and Edition Wortschatz, Schwarzenfeld, Germany.

31. **Landing Rights,** with an illustration by Charles Seliger, Shearsman Books, Bristol, England 2014 and Edition Wortschatz, Schwarzenfeld, Germany.

32. **Listening to Silence,** with an illustration by Charles Seliger, Shearsman Books, Bristol, England 2014 and Edition Wortschatz, Schwarzenfeld, Germany.

33. **Taking Leave,** with an illustration by Mei Fêng, Shearsman Books, Bristol, England 2014 and Edition Wortschatz, Schwarzenfeld, Germany.

34. **Jewel Sensed,** with an illustration by Paul Klee, Shearsman Books, Bristol, England 2015 and Edition Wortschatz, Schwarzenfeld, Germany.

35. **Shadowing Images**, with an illustration by Pieter de Hooch, Shearsman Books, Bristol, England 2015 and Edition Wortschatz, Schwarzenfeld.

36. **Untouched Silences**, with an illustration by Paul Seehaus, Shearsman Books, Bristol, England 2016 and Edition Wortschatz, Schwarzenfeld.

37. **Soundlesss Impressions**, with an illustration by Qi Baishi, Shearsman Books, Bristol, England 2016 and Edition Wortschatz, Schwarzenfeld.

38. **Moon Flowers**, with a photograph by Hannelore Bäumler, Shearsman Books, Bristol, England 2017 and Edition Wortschatz, Schwarzenfeld.

39. **The Healing of a Broken World**, with a photograph by Hannelore Bäumler, Shearsman Books, Bristol, England 2018 and Edition Wortschatz, Cuxhaven.

40. **Opus 40**, with a photograph by Hannelore Bäumler, Shearsman Books, Bristol, England 2018 and Edition Wortschatz, Cuxhaven.

41. **Identity Cause**, with a photograph by Hannelore Bäumler, Shearsman Books, Bristol, England 2018 and Edition Wortschatz, Cuxhaven.

42. **Kaleidoscope**, with a photograph by Hannelore Bäumler, Shearsman Books, Bristol, England 2019 and Edition Wortschatz, Cuxhaven.

43. **Snow-touched Imaginings**, with a photograph by Hannelore Bäumler, Shearsman Books, Bristol, England 2019 and Edition Wortschatz, Cuxhaven.

44. **Two-timed**, with a photograph by Hannelore Bäumler, Shearsman Books, Bristol, England 2020 and Edition Wortschatz, Cuxhaven.

45. **Corona Poems**, with a photograph by Hannelore Bäumler, Shearsman Books, Bristol, England 2020 and Edition Wortschatz, Cuxhaven.

Book on David Jaffin's poetry: Warren Fulton, **Poemed on a beach,** Ahadada, Tokyo, Japan and Toronto, Canada 2010.